C A L I B A N

CALIBAN

poems

john whalen

LOST HORSE PRESS SANDPOINT IDAHO

Versions of some of the poems have appeared in the following magazines:

Turned into a Bird: CUTBANK
Theft: DARK HORSE
Three Yellow Dogs of Sorrow, The Apostles' Fault, Ransom Note, Sweet Accord: HELIOTROPE
Flocking: THE HOLLINS CRITIC
Big: LYRIC: THE CITY LIGHTS POETRY REVIEW
Greenhouse: SCRIPT
Delivery: STRINGTOWN
How to Dance: SWAMP ROOT
Attendants of Grass, Cartography, Courage, In the Forest-Headed Woman, Two Bones: 20 POUNDS OF HEADLIGHTS
Caliban Limb from Limb: UBU
The Beauty of Tactical Surprise, Black Velvet, Chlorophyll Angels: VIRGINIA QUARTERLY REVIEW
How to Seduce a Man: YELLOW SILK
Space Travel, Biggest Living Thing: YAWP
Radio: WILLOW SPRINGS

First line of *Self-Portrait* after Robert Penn Warren.
Caliban Limb From Limb is dedicated to Emily.
In the Forest-Headed Woman is for Max.

Printed in the United States of America.

First Edition

Library of Congress Cataloging-in-Publication Data

Whalen, John, 1957-
Caliban: poems / John Whalen.
p. cm.
ISBN 0-9668612-6-4 (alk. paper)
I. Title.
PS3623.H35 C35 2002
811'.6–dc21

2002001144

ACKNOWLEDGMENTS

Many people have encouraged these poems more than I can say. Thank you to Christine Holbert and Scott Poole for shepherding *Caliban* through publication. They made it look easy. Thank you to my first teachers, Rodney Jones and A.R. Ammons. Thanks to Bruce Holbert for his generosity and intelligence. Thank you to Nance Van Winckel for her kind mentorship and to Christopher Howell for his fine ear. Thank you especially to Max Phillips, always a determined friend of these poems. His insightful editing has strengthened this book.

CONTENTS

CALIBAN

HOUSE OF CALIBAN

CALIBAN LIMB FROM LIMB

THE GREAT HEART MUSCLE

For my daughters, Virginia and Sally

CALIBAN

Thou wert but a lost monster.

–The Tempest

SMALL THINGS

Big Tommy pushes Little Tommy down the stairs.
Little Tommy's the size of a horse but slower.
Sprawled in puddled oil,
he turns to me as if to continue speaking.

Then Big Tommy gets mad
and I have to squinch my eyes at the gravel.

To me he says, "Act good."

The three of us are stocking convenience stores this
summer,
overturning Toyotas,
and bar-hopping to big-screen baseball.

At midnight we head into the hills with whiskey
and cases of ammunition.
We don't like moose interfering with our drinking
with how we want one simple damn thing.

At dawn we're naked, crashing through bushes
into Melanie's back yard.
Small things flail at us with wings as the sun flashes.
I smell fried eggs. Somebody's awake.

Somebody who loves us.

SELF-PORTRAIT

All things lean at me and, though some
mimic the wind, some aim at my teeth.
A pine whips through to my backbone.
Now Caliban can stand straight,
but the five a.m. light gives up on clarity
as night bunches into a western storm.
Whatever I see is gray.
Fortunately, the rain is extravagant.
It howls.
I stand there: needle, bone, heart,
neither reborn, nor disappointed.

HOW TO SEDUCE A MAN

1
The weather interrupted the month-long conversation
about humidity's effect on imagination.
Imagine seventeen battleship-sized clouds
bearing down upon the city. Cool air on their shoulders.
The rigors of weather!

I want to be a lake in the afternoon light
as clouds plan winter with the wind
and Melanie steps off her bike at the shore,
takes off her skirt.

2
Sparkles, flushes, dances, speaks.
Light and voice caught in boxes.
In Bozeman yesterday a farmer shot his T.V.

Above the radar dish: all the proud sky.
But we're hiding behind doors, digging in.
We are not even tall as trees.

In the brilliant television orchard
I'm standing upside down
eating a plum.

I am lost in a plum. I start another.
Lost in a plum.
Stuck in sweet true plumness and the radical light.

Incompletely illuminated, boxed in,
I'm getting poorer. She's getting richer.
I'm certainly getting richer.
I'm a doorknob reflecting a thousand bad decisions,
and there she is down by the water,
converting legs and breasts to large light!

DELIVERY

From the bar to Sixth up the hill from the interstate,
with Tommy drunk across my shoulders, falling,
half-drunk myself, running from a little joke
the sheriff invented to pry my good name
from church-lettering into this crooked rain.

Melanie didn't answer the door, but Tommy stirred,
so I dumped him, skinny crippled nothing,
my only friend, down on stones.
Later, in a room of roses saved from frost,
we circled a failing space heater.

Melanie said to hell with people who never liked us anyway.
My head filled with coffee and flower stink.
On and on she talked, Tommy and I huddled there
in the warm kitchen light. Then Tommy grunted:
through the window we saw the paperboy

jumping up and down on one leg, then the other.
He swung his arm, and more lies broke the glass.
We watched him dance at the center of the grass
under stars bluer than uniforms.

GREENHOUSE

Painters in white caps and shirts
second-coat the outside of the library white
and a green-haired beautician floats up the steps
as you descend, slipping off your heels,
unbuttoning your silk blouse.

In a tank top and running shoes,
you sprint home to prune your seventy-two rose bushes.

My hands dream of reaching around thorns
and rubbing your belly. When I move into the greenhouse,
we'll polish the rise of petal from stem,
lick blood from each other's fingers.

RANSOM NOTE

The line at the bank is slow,
so I hold everyone hostage.

A dull bone, always a beginner,
I sneak out of there with you.
You've never been kidnapped before,
and you don't like it.

I know who I am: twenty-nine stitches
across the head of a friend
and a fear of flowers.

Tiny, unrakeable, dark, the sodden leaves
deserve your attention more than I.

Now you're on about digging out the bones of the lost city
of the land of Apum.
Mesopotamia this. Mesopotamia that.

We have barely six inches clearance
under the gambling tables of morning
as we shoot downhill ahead of the police
into desert and a wide, flaring sun.

I search above traffic for the star you admire.
O, I'm not willing to unilaterally calm down.

RADIO

Even when the change is oblique, unnoticed,
and the wind pulls at the windows facing the creek
like fortune come to yank at a bingo winner,

even when just one book is out of place
or a pot that wasn't
is set inside a larger pot,

you look up,
wondering what has emptied the air.
Not that

as much as what two hands are to each other
in a darkening house
as rain glazes the remaining snow,

and the radio, set too loud, whines.
After you turn it off,
your hand extends into the silence

as if the click of the dial indicated a formal invitation,
as if someone were pointing with cupped fingers
in five directions at once to explain a sudden doubt.

BEAUTIFUL PUNISHMENT

When he first saw your face through the crowd
of usual misfits at the demolition derby,
Caliban closed his eyes
and was taller, cleaner, and smarter.

He followed all evening
the faint fluorescence of your shadow,
moaning when you looked back at him,

ten steps behind you
in the midnight neighborhood,
through the rooms of your house which tamed
Caliban, gave him a fork and spoon,
bolted him to a chair next to yours.

FLOCKING

Heat, hour, motion of the wind there,
fallen trees, green branches among
the men chopping: I cannot forget
that mountain, six hundred miles
and seven months away, a different sky
when the moon comes. People say
winter gets back for every warm day,
but near Bald Mountain and Round Knob
or Horse Creek or Paint Creek
in February, the month I was born,
teenage lovers come to share
blankets under dark rhododendron.

CALIBAN

1. Caliban Writes a Poem
Everything behind the beat station wagon
of my shoulders is shining when you raise the hood.
There's not much of a motor, just oil and dust.

You slide into the driver's seat.
From beneath your Caliban T-shirt,
your right nipple grazes the steering wheel.

Sumac has pushed through the dash,
yet the old Chrysler moans,
the radio barks, and the lone windshield wiper
shudders. Against my usual background

of rust and collision, the light arranges
itself in little spikes.
And you're humming, I think. Humming to me.

2. Voices in My Head
Mr. Caliban thinks he's a car.
And what does he want with a woman?
They say I/you look like a fish.
But I'm no fish. We don't like fish.
And Caliban was the first one

on this true island's circumstance.
I mean the way his mind gnaws on trees,
the easy way in which people hit him.
Caliban knows what happens in the dark
and everything about monsters.
He knows transmissions. Crust of oil.
Terribly chewed again,
Caliban's nights are full of teeth.

JEALOUSY

Frantic because I'm kissing you,
night cannot solve my grin.
Now the moon whistles behind thick sirens
signaling snow.

Night torches my remaining tooth, accidentally
igniting blue sunrise

that leaps aboard my desire for your composure
and the length of your legs.

HOUSE OF CALIBAN

Sometimes a thousand twangling instruments
Will hum about mine ears; and sometimes voices,
That, if I then had waked after long sleep,
Will make me sleep again: and then, in dreaming,
The clouds methought would open, and show riches
Ready to drop upon me; that when I waked
I cried to dream again.

–*The Tempest*

THE APOSTLES' FAULT

Caliban's swallowing a house
in which everything is unpaid for,
all the details to strip, sand and paint.

It's a loved procession
bearing down
like the hoarse gibberish of apostles begging on the street:
isn't it wonderful how everything falls apart?

When I kneel on the lawn, the house rises
sideways into the hill.
Isn't it the apostles' fault?

It's what I told you before, what I always say.
It's not my bad luck so much as a religious event.

DRAWDOWN

On the other side of the Snake River Dam
motorboats used to heckle canoes.
Fifty feet down a cracked bank, drawdown
has exposed a ghost town of bingo parlors,

stoned mechanics, and ex-husbands with big ears.
Past the old grocery, down the dried mud
of the street's dream of giant salmon,
in a basement on Elm I've locked wrenches

with a burst water main. Above me
the house sleeps, the baby sleeps, the dog sleeps.
Upstairs dreaming of bees is a woman
who knows ways under anything she touches

to groundwater. She dreams a blind man tending hives:
under backlit, purple clouds, a sudden storm
unbuttons dimness from his eyes. Through miraculously
    pissed bees,
he sees his first warm rain swallow the streets.

THEFT

It's not that going up into a willow tree
will stop the birds in my head from their racket,
but all across the water is the light
flashing sun prints in the wake of motorboats.

A black family is fishing off the point,
where bass come to trade for cheese and night crawlers,
stealing from loose lines.

When I dive, my arc becomes
a kind of bartered theft. As I stole
the willow's height, I take this water,
this nakedness, for my own.

RELIGION

now you call a person faggot and he sends
you a postcard from bessemer, alabama where
secretly he's been attending revivals
with station wagons full of baptists
and says his yellow horse found a field
which jumps out of the way
when you yell jesus christ is coming
and the clouds thunder etc

BIG

I was stalled at Buffalo and Aurora
when this fat woman bounced across the street
and motioned me to try again.
Big. Big.
She crouched down, lifted
the back of the station wagon and ran.
I jump-started from second gear.
I felt her hands on my bumper for a month.

MANSION OF NOISE

Centered upon an irritated buzz
wound across the daily household roar,
the anniversary of our first kiss
obliques through chores and kids.

And swim lessons. Abandoned cars we're still paying for
nudge our neighborhood downward. Day punches
ear-shattering day. I like it,
scrunched up tight against you

in the middle of whine and whistle.
Then the blare, and it won't ever stop for us.
Cars growl up Cedar. Lawn mowers race more
rain. Kids hammer driftwood modifications

to a blue tree house. Loud-spiked floor, forested
roof, walls of leaves thick as your hair.

PRAYED RAIN

Heat wave breaks
in the form of a giant-wheeled pickup
arriving late in prayed rain.

Compressors start up.
Men jackhammer our front steps.

By dark the lawn's a mess,
and concrete's piled in the street,
sloppy gray chunks of it.

We climb to the top
and rightly blame three weeks of sharp talk
on the drought on the burned grass on the neighbor's new car.

I propose
you put down that chocolate.
Balance it on concrete,
anywhere in the drizzle.

When we kiss, the rubble
shifts beneath us. It's necessary
to keep my hand slapping
against the good hum of my heart.

HERE'S A HOUSE

Awake all night as wind screeched through trees,
I rise at dawn. Melanie hasn't stirred
nor broken any new promises.
Ignoring the kitchen, a mess of last night's rice

and ice cream scum, I wrestle memories
of an open-shirted breast glimpsed accidentally.
Light off the remembered nipple
expands until chairs and table bruise

with the icy patina of how
I've been cautioned, captured, wakened
by the smell of another woman's skin.
Here's a house she'll never enter.

GREGOR SAMSA

In my dream your right hand's a crab, the yard's
thirsty, and the washing machine's unbalanced:
a small roar pulls at the rumbling quiet.
Pipes shudder toward sprinkler heads. Heavy
flowers peck low windows. And there's something
I don't want to tell you—sugared coffee
stained your Basic Kafka. As Gregor Samsa
awoke one morning from uneasy dreams

he found himself transformed in his bed
into a gigantic insect. And if
we spin him on the butt of his shell, he'll
rock to the sprinkler's unforgiving
beat: an underside of the lives upstairs.
A peony hugging the dirt under flower-weight.
The washer's shrill alarm that it's done.

MY ORIGINAL FUTURE

1
I leave the donut shop
and drive to an early morning volunteer guard shift
at a church targeted by the self-proclaimed "Arsonist of
God,"

who has burned three churches in three weeks.
I will cut through the nine conformations of the dark.
Caliban disguised as rain.

2
Big plans have drilled a homicidal dullness
into my ears. In the farm of cars
my mother calls home,
all the hillbillies in my family are forever
rigging carburetors, switching batteries,
or trading tires between wrecks.

They roll somehow into town and park
along the calm, clean street in front of my house.

Soon dozens of them straddle chairs,
their big feet in my daughters' plastic pool.
Everyone howls at the intermittent neighborhood traffic.
Under perfect skies, they drool
and pull up the grass and look just like me.

CHLOROPHYLL ANGELS

When it rains, the county sands our road
with cat litter. Later, clay pellets melt
around the inner shells of grass seed.

By morning the road needs a trim.
Tommy hooks up the triple
blade to his John Deere 214.

Set too low, the blade cuts deeper
than green, uncovering the white roots
of chlorophyll angels at choir practice.

When he's done, mower in the shed,
shed door locked and polished, you can hear
the angels: *swing low* sounds like

the reluctant, yet hopeful, footsteps
of beginning divers climbing their first cliff
above the wide, unpredictable green.

CALIBAN LIMB FROM LIMB

And that most deeply to consider is
The beauty of his daughter.

The spirit torments me: –O!

–*The Tempest*

SWEET ACCORD

Everything's south of excitement,
south of blond. In everything
you said I searched for sweet accord.

Don't look for me now out your sour window
or at the kissed tips of your ears.
Flu has scratched my throat

and the snow has placed itself
on each trim branch and car wreck.
When sun roars, I shout what I recall of you

at the porch of mother's illegal dump
and its chromatic sky. O sun, most lit and most smart!
I don't anymore want anything.

IN THE FOREST-HEADED WOMAN

The granite bedrock begs for distraction,
but the river stops short of town
when she climbs my back teeth again

with a drill and a curved-claw hammer.
A four-alarm fire surprises Market Street
in the heat of everyone watching the heel of her hand.

She kneads the back of my head with the rolling
thumb motion of a female serial killer
hitchhiking a black pickup off Interstate 80.

The truck lists slightly to the left.
A front-end alignment problem
that won't be repaired by the present owner.

CARTOGRAPHY

And here you are with me,
the middle of the water

with the reflection of sky,
reflected trees, clouds.

Here your shadow turns
as you turn, yawns, shuffles away.

Inside you then your strong donkey
stomps.

My shoes galloping back
and back along the back roads.

COURAGE

On a table wedged between four spruce
you pour water from a bucket to a bowl,
set the surface on fire, and blind every germ in the yard.
Now you can eat.

Don't you remember when we owned the entire hill
and nothing was far away?

But we deeded the rain and bright blue barns
to strangers, then moved west
where our gestures, especially, are incomplete.

When I point toward the grocery
(I might be going! To buy cantaloupe!),
an airless courage beats me back indoors.
In a new cleanliness ritual you burn

three holes in the floor, then patch them
with green linoleum.

But when I twist myself against you
in the wild spit of rain, we accommodate each other,
drown as the neighborhood drowns.

CALIBAN LIMB FROM LIMB

You said there was a mix-up in the shadows
of some trees where an approaching shadow dissolves
and a darker, second shadow appears to carry the absent light.
At this spot both shadows hesitate

to see which way you'll turn.
You said your walk with those shadows
was your own motion mapped elastically.
Chasing me is the way you did not turn.

A shadow of yours I saw too much, sprinting
downhill behind me everywhere,
is your nightly run in the repetition of nights:
the wrong shadow carrying the dark with dark gloves.

THE BEAUTY OF TACTICAL SURPRISE

Funny, that you too hired the assassin
who has made such a mess of the woods.

I wanted to believe in second chance. I wanted honesty.
When I could no longer pray, I borrowed fifty bucks

to employ a truthteller to hum the locust song
of our confusions. I showed him our letters.

He examined our photographs and toiletries,
as I muttered about the landscape between us.

He advertised my love at garage sales.
He hosted a picnic you never attended.

You couldn't forgive the plumbing or the weather or me.
Now you march like an army one hundred miles a day

because you are hypnotized by the beauty of tactical surprise,
unconcerned with the soldiers' feet which bloom

and blister in the blue heat your discomfort ignites.
A flood swallows the somnambulant creek

and bulldozers follow the assassin's search
for evidence of our affection, its radical gesture.

ROCK FIGHTS

Without you, my chest swamps with bile.
I dream of rock fights and parasites.
A murdered child haunts me awake from a dream.
Under the shower in the harsh bathroom
I pray for pretty new days.
My hoarse lungs sound like tankers
stocking the swamp again. Without you,
the crew has cheap maps. The directions are false,
the coordinates bad guesses of drunk surveyors:
the dreamed child our failure together.

MAYBE THIS FEAR

Maybe this vinegar piling my thoughts
like steel girders
in the insomniac rain

will fall through doubt
I can't answer, and I will sleep again,
innocent of your moods.

You suspect bitterness everywhere.
It follows you,
a bulldog's jaw attached

to grace you won't acknowledge.
If the hike home drains enough sourness,
you could wrap and send yourself

UPS to Australia
where it all hasn't already turned,
hard cider when your tongue wants cake.

BLACK VELVET

A truck with Georgia plates
unloaded a ton of velvet onto the traffic island
between Route 13 and the Elmira Road.

Across the street in wind and rain
I'm attaching seats to chains on swing sets.
The sky is a sprung leak.

How I forget the details of our love!
Your face like a desert
or a municipal drought.

The sun escapes some thunder
to follow an old black man who squeezes
his voice out from behind a cigar

to praise the concrete steps
and northwest clouds, the carriers of water.

AFFECTION

When you kicked a soccer ball from between my feet,
I fell.
When you juggled two water glasses one-handed
and made one disappear, that was a trick to forget me.

The discarded affection around this house
has tainted the well water, splintered the barn.

I never thought you'd call a taxi
to take you from these sullen pines
to the county airport just ahead
of a blizzard that can't quite catch your plane.

Not that current events don't ponder you.
Wind arrives. Cars won't start.
Trucks overturn in your anger.
What frustrates you confuses nations.

A chimney fire licks at the roof.
Maybe you don't think of me at all.

ATTENDANTS OF GRASS

Forest-fire smoke from British Columbia
has dirtied another evening here
in a neighborhood you've probably forgotten:
frame houses lined under Douglas firs,

and, scuttling everywhere, attendants of grass:
lawn technicians with whom we barbecued and gossiped
a domestic life you fled. I don't blame
absence or richer love. It's just that

I'm sunk lower than the Spokane River
drowning itself in channels bit deep in better years
of snowmelt, better evenings

when we'd turn off the TV, aim the fan at the table
and sit counting pennies into red wrappers.
You dressed in hiking boots and nothing else.

THREE YELLOW DOGS OF SORROW

If you quit smoking,
but I'm still hiding somewhere
inside your pine-scented car,
does a shout explain me?
Or rain,

does rain remember the wrong river
of me slipping down hills sharper
than animals no one has ever touched?

It's true, your shoulders blossom
and blossom, and the restaurant rattles
in the storm of a train.
But I never should have talked to you.

Three yellow dogs track me
across parking lots and uprooted streets.
I walk on my hands,
but I can't shout anymore.
Not your name.

TWO BONES

Out of the death of the dinosaurs, flutes
rush to plant chestnuts and willows
on the road to King Ferry in 1801.
Months of heavy snow had deepened
the mud under a lingering smell of gunpowder and root.

Melanie, can't we discuss your native disposition?
Speak again of the zodiacal lights?
Squinting and complaining, I wander my mistrust
of solid objects toward no new business.

In the next movement violins scratch my face
like the wind from Lake Ontario contracts my two bones:
brain and heart.
I play them for what they're worth.

BIGGEST LIVING THING

After our divorce
anger, impatience, and inertia
scared me into the hospital again.

The nurses ignored me.
The doctors only asked can you bend your knee
like this, like that.

My daughter drew a giant sequoia for me.
The biggest living thing, she said,
272 feet high and 3500 years old.

Back home, I transplanted
a forty-five foot maple
from the side yard to the kitchen,

cut a hole through the ceiling
into the second floor bedroom, and
shot the top of the tree out the roof

I built window boxes and planted poplars,
juniper, Arizona cypress and purple-leafed filbert.
The neighbors formed a committee.

My picture was in the paper:
disheveled, bearded, dumbstruck.
The next day, my birthday,

I shaved and put on a white shirt.
You were dropping off boxes of clothes
and paperbacks when it began to rain.

I mean the sprinklers started up.
I said you smelled different.
You said, no, Caliban.

I grabbed you: sassafras, beech, Carolina hemlock.
The mild forests of our hair
braided together like knuckles.

TURNED INTO A BIRD

Your letter asking twenty-five dollars
slept in my pocket a week
before turning into a bird who shouted "Hurrah"

in front of Gunther's Grocery. The men
and their dogs were confused, as was I.
We all began barking, the red dusk came.

When that bird became night on wings,
the mountains reddened, we stopped
our circling, dogs became birds.

If you had seen everything red as it was
when the dusk flew, if you had seen the stone
houses and girls on porches, quiet,

red as cut cedar along gullies, on top of the hills,
you would have flown into a bird with me,
now traveling, now diving.

THE GREAT HEART MUSCLE

Sometime am I
All wound with adders, who with cloven tongues
Do hiss me into madness.

Beat him enough: after a little time,
I'll beat him too.

–*The Tempest*

THE GREAT HEART MUSCLE

No actual birds, skittish and hungry,
fly within me the sleepless night
and wake early near water.

The great heart muscle
murmurs your name, searches
behind tree-shadowed buildings for you.

Along the ground and white brick
of the bakery, color questions me brightly:
lemons of the flower alphabet—a wealth

of incomprehensible pastels:
where are you if you are not
stalking Caliban?

I have lost your smell
and a sense which we shared
of rain following rain

the afternoons we tasted
each other's skin.
Dust of sun after a storm,

I am a strong man in a circus
poster. Ruin me until I am wrong
and cold as you are.

WALLPAPERING THE ASYLUM

Tommy ran off soon as he reached the road,
then escaped down to Binghamton, while the rest
of us inmates grouped outside to gawk
at the Russians on the moon and the jokers on Mars.

Yeah, I knew he had that turbo-charged,
4-wheel-drive jeep up his sleeve
and freedom stuck in his throat.

Clock and refrigerator clack, whir, hum
to wake the morning fog into snow.
Even with the microscope my mother sent
and its advantages for self-examination, nothing changes.

Breakfast cleaned up, water box ready,
Fred Lee is cutting strips of wallpaper for the corners.
Here Johnson still gives the orders.
Glue drips from his chin.

Paper sky and rodeo, screaming birds and three clouds.
Then again, paper sky and rodeo.

Me, I want to be like Tommy.
Strong, like a Canadian snowstorm

pushing south into warmer air.
To slam from ice into lightning.
Finish decorating these walls with an ax,
sit down with the gasping sun and the black constellations.

ANOTHER LOOSE WILLOW

There goes a tornado, thunder, and another loose willow.
There goes everyone down to the donut shop in the rain.
Antonio is smoking Marlboros with his honey glaze,
and no one speaks to me
because I am slave, a greasy old tree,
because whatever hurts
positions itself perfectly for rain when the rain won't quit.
Whatever's hurt: ripped, raised, rescued.

CAVE DRAWINGS

Caliban admires a naked woman,
my wife eating breakfast.
On an island neglected by sweet smells,
what can a shoe-string budget afford?
Caliban wants the fat snow to cover everything,
even his lack of sleep
which he calls a victory.
How many dark trees constitute
a tattooed heart pierced by a bone?
His biceps readies for a kiss.
How many fat days before she speaks again
of his charm?
Caliban boils chicken soup.
He's all dressed up
in a cave where he's drawn all the walls.

PRESENT DOUBT

Tomorrow I begin to wish that the geology
always involving me in repair of rotting wall struts
and dangerously slick friendships
would violently quake.

There are ten houses in the gracious valley.
I found a partial deck
card by card in the leaves.
Finished with the chores of emptiness,
I deal two hands of chance and slender ankles.

I bet a faltered wall between the oaks.
The past bets a swamp where stories invent memory
to defend present doubt. I draw an ace, my third.

The past draws one to fill a flush.

Sick of losing, I feint to the left
where failure had beaten a track, jump back
into the quicksand.
Leave standing upright.

A swamp chews what it cannot swallow whole.
I coast green into the valley toward shining houses.

SPACE TRAVEL

Name is Mud.
Family name Mud. Town name Mud.
I've got callused hands, weird mind.

There is a thickness to the air in this town,
men hiding behind buildings,
someone riding a blue bicycle in the rain.

Fog's for breakfast,
anesthesia all afternoon, TV for dinner.
Tonight they're launching spaceships.

There are close-ups of the sky!
Oh, "space travel" is a pretty saying,
like "summer" or "pre-approved."

Next-door is a moose painted pink.
Lawn forms and a radar dish in every yard.
Name is Mud and, yes, it's a pretty saying,

"s p a c e t r a v e l,"
one that does not mire itself on a furry tongue.
They are shining, slippery words,

far apart, yet personal,
as if Mud could escape town
running, leaping on his padded and thorough hands

across moonlit blacktop, through exhausted
suburbs and shopping plazas,
through the dangerous highway verbs and the nouns of leaving.

Space travel, space travel! Damn!
Mud's life is super-glued to a truncated Volkswagen van
hauling a swimming pool across town,

and my times are not those of an American hero.
But space travel! I'm talking about far away and lean
and sitting cool and fooling around with telescopes!

Yes, if just once Caliban could step far enough away
to look back at the earth reflecting the sun
like a flipped coin, smooth and heartening as a nickel.

HOW TO DANCE

1.

Between heads in the afternoon,
Big Tommy, barber,
picks the thin triggers of his banjo.

Milk, eggs, bread. Milk, eggs, bread.
All the people walking in the front door
don't know the weight they are dragging

is their own secret seal skin.
And if they go tonight to a cliff overlooking water,
turn around and pry the possibility

of new skin over their heads,
then they could stretch into a weight
they've always been afraid of

and dive out as far as the drunk moon,
dive forthrightly.
Out here in the water, it's always dancing weather.

2.

Wrench-gut bellow of machine
dragging behind me like a singed tail,
after work I stop at the lake.

An hour under water
and I'm alone: convicted
of myself, forgiven and howling again

as the drunk moon rises
over silver city lights.
No matter how fast you go,

when you get there
the future offers familiar trees.
Naturally, Caliban's initials

are scratched into the sidewalk
in front of the house
where everyone is whistling on the porch.

BROKEN JAW

Caliban falls out of bed to sit by the window
like everyone said not to.
Immediately, his eyes feel better,
as if someone had cleaned spit from his hornrims.

He can see low clouds
and a hundred-foot-high sun against the aluminum sky.
He watches the trees darken like cast-iron pots,
and, leaning out the window too far,
shouts at the geese on their way to the county dump.

The back lawn jumps up to visit him,
and later a doctor visits his mother.
She says, oh, he's a real rocket scientist.
Caliban disagrees, but where he lives,
they don't like noise.
They clamp his jaw with barbed wire.

And no one guesses his resolve to escape.
To touch the velvet bushes with his good hand,
the one he never chewed.

At dawn his grin buckles steel.
As if remembering an appointment, he staggers
outside where the sun is jumping.
Vexed angels clutter the peripheral world.

NOBODY

I warned you and kissed and kicked you,
but you pile good deeds like grain
against future poverty. You
lock your door and chain

yourself above the grit
of the unplanned.
You want everything proper and stark:
gray on gray jammed

onto your marriage like a concussion.
You aim your hunger along the spine
of virtue's perfect mission.
But when your mood's in line

with the equinox, it'll be too late for us.
Creeping through fields of anger,
I scrub, scour, and fuss.
Me and you, we feed the drunk rangers

of the soup kitchen on a Friday gone bodacious.
When you leave, I bike
the dead snow, breathing rough.
There isn't anyone like

me chasing you: nobody's at your house
and nobody's in your bedroom
when I put on your dress, joust
with the mirror. Love is groomed

excitement, a complex lie
of getting to know you. Love is difficult weather.
A bruised feather
of pigment in the corner of my eye.

SAINT LOST

Blind, roughly coffined in a suit,
when I shout for you,
I learn no one's in my country.

Why are we stuck at this funeral
without the least drunken brawl or bright skirt
if you know these pilgrims all by name?

Exiled to nights of counterfeiting,
dumb, lustful, I lived the best I could.
For you, Saint Lost, for you.

Don't bury me halfheartedly.
My crime, didn't I live? I beg you.
Take my hand! Shuffle your feet.

That's it, waltz.
Are you as light as I am? Admit it.
Now, let's get out of here.

O this must be what I wanted to be doing:
pulling you up stairs built into the hill
from the top of which one can see Montana

and Spain. Let's plant a flag.
Another waltz? Hunkered, moping but moving.
Enough of a waltz.

ABOUT THE AUTHOR

John Whalen lives in Eastern Washington with his two daughters. He works as a sales rep for a computer security consultancy. His poems have appeared in such journals as the *Virginia Quarterly Review*, *Yellow Silk*, *The Hollins Critic*, *Willow Springs*, and *CutBank*.